THE CHINESE HOROSCOPES LIBRARY

RABBIT

KWOK MAN-HO

DORLING KINDERSLEY
LONDON • NEW YORK • STUTTGART

A DORLING KINDERSLEY BOOK

Senior Editor   Sharon Lucas
Art Editor   Camilla Fox
Managing Editor   Krystyna Mayer
Managing Art Editor   Derek Coombes
DTP Designer   Doug Miller
Production Controller   Antony Heller

Artworks: Danuta Mayer 4, 8, 11, 17, 27, 29, 31, 33, 35;
Giuliano Fornari 21; Jane Thomson; Sarah Ponder.

Special Photography by Steve Gorton. Thank you to The British Museum, Chinese Post
Office, Percival David Foundation of Chinese Art, and The Powell-Cotton Museum.

Additional Photography: Eric Crichton, Jo Foord, Steve Gorton, Dave King, Martin Norris,
Tim Ridley.

Picture Credits: Circa Photo Library 12, 18; Percival David Foundation of Chinese Art 23bl,
Royal Geographical Society 25tr.

First published in Great Britain in 1994
by Dorling Kindersley Limited,
9 Henrietta Street, London WC2E 8PS

Copyright © 1994 Dorling Kindersley Limited, London
Text copyright © 1994 ICOREC

A CIP catalogue record for this book is available from the British Library

ISBN 0-7513-0119-1

Reproduced by GRB Editrice, Verona, Italy
Printed and bound in Hong Kong by Imago

CONTENTS

Introducing Chinese Horoscopes 8

Casting your Horoscope 10

Myths and Legends 12

Personality 14

Love 16

Career 18

Health 20

Leisure 22

Symbolism 24

Buddha Rabbit 26

Rabbit Looking at the Moon 28

Rabbit Running Out of the
Forest 30

Rabbit in the Burrow 32

Rabbit Running In the Forest .. 34

Your Chinese Month of Birth .. 36

Your Chinese Day of Birth 38

Your Chinese Hour of Birth 40

Your Fortune in other Animal
Years 42

Your Chinese Year of Birth 44

INTRODUCING CHINESE HOROSCOPES

For thousands of years, the Chinese have used their astrology and religion to establish a harmony between people and the world around them.

The exact origins of the twelve animals of Chinese astrology – the Rat, Ox, Tiger, Rabbit, Dragon, Snake, Horse, Ram, Monkey, Rooster, Dog, and Pig – remain a mystery. Nevertheless, these animals are important in Chinese astrology. They are much more than general signposts to the year, and to the possible good or bad times ahead for us all. The twelve animals of Chinese astrology are considered to be a reflection of the Universe itself.

YIN AND YANG SYMBOL
White represents the female force of yin, and black represents the masculine force of yang.

every single thing in the Universe is held in balance by the dynamic, cosmic forces of yin and yang. Yin is feminine, watery, and cool; the force of the Moon and the rain. Yang is masculine, solid, and hot; the force of the Sun and the Earth. According to ancient Chinese belief, the concentrated essences of yin and yang became the four seasons, and the scattered essences of yin and yang became the myriad creatures that are found on Earth.

The twelve animals of Chinese astrology are all associated with either yin or yang. The forces of yin rise as winter approaches. These forces decline with the warmth of spring, when yang begins to assert

YIN AND YANG
The many differences in our natures, moods, health, and fortunes reflect the wider changes within the Universe. The Chinese believe that

itself. Even in the course of a normal day, yin and yang are at work, constantly changing and balancing. These forces also naturally rise and fall within us all.

Everyone has their own internal balance of yin and yang. This affects our tempers, ambitions, and health. We also respond to the changes of weather, to the environment, and to the people who surround us.

THE FIVE ELEMENTS

All that we can touch, taste, or see is divided into five basic types or elements – wood, fire, earth, gold, and water. Everything in the Universe can be linked to one of these elements.

For example, the element wood is linked to the Tiger and to the Rabbit. This element is also linked to the colour green, sour-tasting food, the season of spring, and the

emotion of anger. The activity of these elements indicates the fortune that may befall us.

AN INDIVIDUAL DISCOVERY

Chinese astrology can help you balance your yin and yang. It can also tell you which element you are, and the colours, tastes, parts of the body, or emotions that are linked to your particular sign. Your fortune can be prophesied according to the year, month, day, and hour in which you were born. You can identify the type of people to whom you are attracted, and the career that will suit your character. You can understand your changes of mood, your reactions to other places, and to other people. In essence, you can start to discover what makes you an individual.

DIVINATION STICKS
Another ancient and popular method of Chinese fortune-telling is using special divination sticks to obtain a specific reading from prediction books.

CASTING YOUR HOROSCOPE

*The Chinese calendar is based on the movement of the
Moon, unlike the calendar used in the Western world,
which is based on the movement of the Sun.*

Before you begin to cast your
Chinese horoscope, check your year
of birth on the chart on pages 44 to
45. Check particularly carefully if
you were born in the early months of
the year. The Chinese year does not
usually begin until January or
February, and you might belong to
the previous Chinese year. For
example, if you were born in 1961
you might assume that you were
born in the Year of the Ox.
However, if your birthday falls
before 15 February you belong to the
previous Chinese year, which is the
Year of the Rat.

THE SIXTY-YEAR CYCLE
The Chinese measure the passing of
time by cycles of sixty years. The
twelve astrological animals appear
five times during the sixty-year
cycle, and they appear in a slightly
different form every time. For
example, if you were born in 1951

you are a Rabbit in the Burrow, but
if you were born in 1963, you are a
Rabbit Running in the Forest.

MONTHS, DAYS, AND HOURS
The twelve lunar months of the
Chinese calendar do not correspond
exactly with the twelve Western
calendar months. This is because
Chinese months are lunar, whereas
Western months are solar. Chinese
months are normally twenty-nine to
thirty days long, and every three to
four years an extra month is added to
keep approximately in step with the
Western year.

One Chinese hour is equal to two
Western hours, and the twelve
Chinese hours correspond to the
twelve animal signs.

The year, month, day, and hour
of birth are the keys to Chinese
astrology. Once you know them,
you can start to unlock your personal
Chinese horoscope.

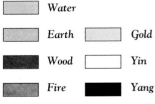

Water

Earth Gold

Wood Yin

Fire Yang

CHINESE ASTROLOGICAL WHEEL
In the centre of the wheel is the yin and yang symbol. It is surrounded by the Chinese astrological character linked to each animal. The band of colour reveals your element, and the outer ring shows whether you are yin or yang.

MYTHS AND LEGENDS

According to Chinese legend, the Jade Emperor, the ruler of Heaven, asked to see the Earth's twelve most interesting animals, then awarded the Rabbit fourth place.

The rabbit is a symbol of longevity, and is believed to live in the Moon, where it slowly grinds the Pill of Immortality with a pestle and mortar. There is an ancient Chinese belief that only female rabbits existed. They were thought to become pregnant by eating plant shoots, and to give birth by spitting their young from their mouths.

BUDDHA AND THE RABBIT

Long ago, the Buddha came to a remote forest. He had travelled for many days, and was tired and hungry. The animals of the forest were all determined to serve him in the best possible way. They gathered together, and decided to find food for him. Each animal brought the food that it naturally harvested.

The rabbit thought of bringing some grass. "I like grass," thought the rabbit, "so I expect the Buddha will, too." So he found a patch of fresh,

THE MOON GODDESS
The gods carried Princess Sheung Ngao to the Moon to escape her violent husband. She lives there with the rabbit, shown on the bottom left of this Chinese tablet.

RABBIT MIRROR

This bronze mirror shows the rabbit using a pestle and mortar to grind the Pill of Immortality. It derives from the Sung dynasty (960–1279).

green grass and started to eat it. When the whole patch was gone, the rabbit suddenly realized what he had done. Next he found some succulent leaves to bring to the Buddha. "After all," said the rabbit, "I like leaves, so I expect the Buddha will, too." He started to eat, and soon there was not a leaf in sight.

Crestfallen, the rabbit brought himself before the Buddha. "O Buddha," said the rabbit, "I am a foolish creature and have nothing to give you except myself. Please eat me if you are hungry." The Buddha was touched by the rabbit's willingness to give up his own life. He placed his hand on the rabbit, and the rabbit flew up to the Moon.

Here, the Buddha set him down, and explained that he would be seen for the rest of time by those on the Earth looking at the Moon.

The Buddha had given the rabbit the supreme gift of eternal life. Even today, if you look at the Moon, you will see the rabbit, forever grinding the Pill of Immortality.

· RABBIT ·
PERSONALITY

The Rabbit has a tranquil and generous character, and a youthful and imaginative outlook. It is sensitive, and is happiest when it is in harmony with its environment.

Your moods are easily affected by people, objects, or the environment in which you find yourself. You can only relax once you have checked everything out to your satisfaction.

MOTIVATION
When people are spurred into action by exciting opportunities and challenges, you tend to hold yourself back until you are absolutely sure what lies ahead. Conflict and aggression make you nervous. You much prefer to remain in the background, rather than taking the limelight. It is only when you are cornered that you attack – if there is the remotest possibility of an escape route, you will take it immediately.

THE INNER RABBIT
You are happiest when the troubles of your everyday life are behind you, and when you feel secure. However, sometimes security can be a little too safe, and there is a possibility that you will miss out on very

PORCELAIN RABBIT
The fine brush strokes and natural colouring on this Chinese porcelain rabbit give it an astonishingly lifelike appearance.

JUMPING RABBITS
This highly coloured porcelain plate depicts five rabbits in autumn. Four rabbits are jumping around the outer rim, and one rabbit is feeding in the centre. The plate dates from the Ch'ing dynasty of 19th-century China.

positive opportunities. Your overriding need for security can make you obstinate. Luckily, when your friends need help you are always there, as long as your moral principles are not remotely compromised.

Your warmth and hospitality are enhanced by your excellent sense of refinement, and when you feel at ease in company you are charming, elegant, and well informed.

Hospitality is one of your natural talents – you are rarely happier than when you are at home entertaining your friends. You are faithful, agreeable, and easy-going. In emotional relationships you are a loving partner, but your tenderness must be returned. You are equally loving and caring in a parental role, but you are not always confident about the best way to cope with the domestic and emotional upheavals of everyday family life.

THE RABBIT CHILD
The young Rabbit is pleasant, obedient, and hardworking. It is often bashful and reticent, and will need plenty of love and encouragement to develop its confidence.

· RABBIT ·
LOVE

The Rabbit loves to be loved, and needs to be treated with care. It is easily upset by erratic passions, and is happiest when it is sustaining a peaceful relationship.

When you find yourself attracted to someone, you are not afraid to show your kindness and affection, for this is your way of winning the object of your desires. If your tenderness is returned, both you and the relationship will blossom, but if you do not receive constant, loving care, the relationship will fade.

You are sensitive, and if you find yourself in an emotional conflict that cannot be resolved, your health is likely to suffer. In the search for a committed relationship you may appear to be fickle, but you are simply testing various relationships until you are sure that

you have found the right partner. Once you have found a soulmate, you are devoted, and find the mere thought of parting virtually unbearable.

Ideally, you are suited to the Pig or the Ram. You share a love of peace, solitude, and honesty with the Pig, but it might prove too outrageous for your conservative nature. The creative and imaginative Ram also wants a peaceful

GODDESS OF LOVE
Kuan Yin is a powerful figure in Chinese mythology. Once a male Buddhist deity, she is now known as the goddess of mercy, and as Sung-tzu, the giver of children.

16

CHINESE COMPATIBILITY WHEEL

Find your animal sign, then look for the animals that share its background colour – the Rabbit has a green background, and is most compatible with the Ram and the Pig. The symbol in the centre of the wheel represents double happiness.

life, and you should bring security and seriousness to the relationship.

The Monkey's wily ways and good advice will be greatly enjoyed by you, and the Monkey will appreciate your discretion and sympathetic nature. The warmth and passion of the Horse could attract you, and you can offer it your ample resources of comfort and love. The Snake shares your love of peace

ORCHID

In China, the orchid, or Lan Hua, is an emblem of love and beauty. It is also a fertility symbol, and represents many offspring.

and beauty, and you will be able to teach it tolerance. The Dog seeks security, and you should find its protective, honest nature appealing.

The Rat's excessive emotions are likely to disturb your precious tranquillity, but a relationship with another Rabbit is likely to be too quiet and peaceful for both of you. The energy of the charismatic Dragon could be irritating, and you may find that your patience is easily exhausted by the excitable and exhibitionistic Rooster.

17

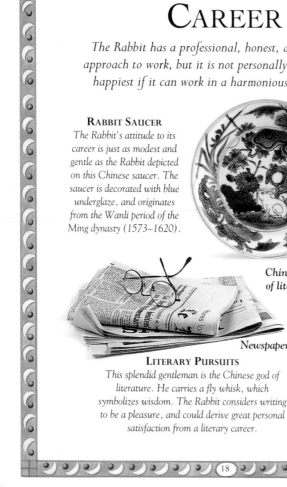

· RABBIT ·
CAREER

*The Rabbit has a professional, honest, and meticulous
approach to work, but it is not personally ambitious. It is
happiest if it can work in a harmonious environment.*

RABBIT SAUCER

*The Rabbit's attitude to its
career is just as modest and
gentle as the Rabbit depicted
on this Chinese saucer. The
saucer is decorated with blue
underglaze, and originates
from the Wanli period of the
Ming dynasty (1573–1620).*

Chinese
porcelain
saucer

Chinese god
of literature

Newspapers

LITERARY PURSUITS

*This splendid gentleman is the Chinese god of
literature. He carries a fly whisk, which
symbolizes wisdom. The Rabbit considers writing
to be a pleasure, and could derive great personal
satisfaction from a literary career.*

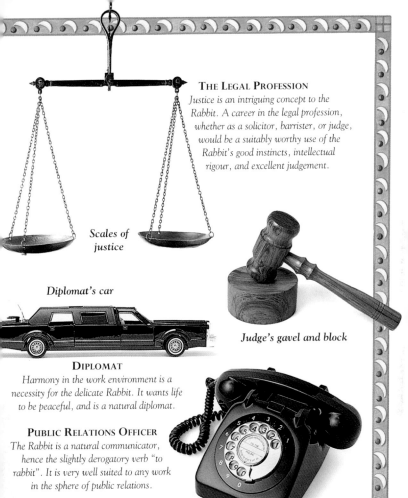

THE LEGAL PROFESSION
Justice is an intriguing concept to the Rabbit. A career in the legal profession, whether as a solicitor, barrister, or judge, would be a suitably worthy use of the Rabbit's good instincts, intellectual rigour, and excellent judgement.

Scales of justice

Diplomat's car

Judge's gavel and block

DIPLOMAT
Harmony in the work environment is a necessity for the delicate Rabbit. It wants life to be peaceful, and is a natural diplomat.

PUBLIC RELATIONS OFFICER
The Rabbit is a natural communicator, hence the slightly derogatory verb "to rabbit". It is very well suited to any work in the sphere of public relations.

Bakelite telephone

HEALTH

Yin and yang are in a continual state of flux within the body. Good health is dependent upon the balance of yin and yang being constantly harmonious.

There is a natural minimum and maximum level of yin and yang in the human body. The body's energy is known as ch'i, and is a yang force. The movement of ch'i in the human body is complemented by the movement of blood, which is a yin force. The very slightest displacement of the balance of yin or yang in the human body can quickly lead to poor health. Yang illness can be cured by yin treatment, and yin illness can be cured by yang treatment.

Everybody has their own individual balance of yin and yang. It is likely that a hot-tempered person will have strong yang forces, and that a more peaceful person will have strong yin forces. Before Chinese medicine can ever be prescribed, your moods have to be carefully taken into account. A balance of joy, anger, sadness, happiness, worry, pensiveness, and fear must be maintained. This fine balance is known as the Harmony of the Seven Sentiments.

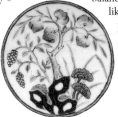

LINGCHIH FUNGUS
The fungus shown in this detail from a Ch'ing dynasty bowl is the "immortal" lingchih fungus, which symbolizes longevity.

CARDAMOM
This aromatic, pleasant-tasting East Indian plant is related to the ginger family.

Born in the Year of the Rabbit, you are associated with the element wood. This element is linked with the liver, gall bladder, tendons, and eyes. These are the parts of the human body that are most relevant to the pattern of your health. You are also associated with the emotion of anger, and with sour-tasting food.

The fruit cardamom (*Elettaria cardamomum*) is associated with your Chinese astrological sign. It is often ground and used as a flavouring, and its seeds can be used as a spice. Cardamom is both yin and yang, and is consequently prescribed for its warming and cooling properties. It is reputed to be a restorer of balance, and can renew the body's vitality. It is also used to calm nausea, and to prevent vomiting.

The use of Chinese medicine is highly specific, therefore never take cardamom or any other plant unless you are following professional advice from a fully qualified Chinese or Western doctor.

ASTROLOGY AND ANATOMY
Your element, wood, is particularly associated with the liver and the gall bladder. The liver is a yin organ, and the gall bladder is a yang organ.

· RABBIT ·
LEISURE

*The Rabbit is a friendly, sociable creature. It enjoys
taking part in many activities, but tends to avoid
any pastimes that involve an element of risk.*

Cricket ball,
bails, stumps,
and bat

TABLE TENNIS
As long as other
people organize and
direct an activity, such
as table tennis, the
Rabbit is more than
happy to join in.

Early table
tennis, or
"ping-pong",
equipment

CRICKET
The Rabbit is fairly
conservative, and
enjoys watching and
playing traditional
sports such as cricket.

Elegant shoes

DRESSING UP

The Rabbit is renowned for its excellent dress sense, and will seize the opportunity to express it. Dinner parties, or any intimate gatherings with friends, are a double source of pleasure for the Rabbit – not only can it dress up in its favourite clothes, but it can also enjoy the company of others.

Material swatches

Chinese rabbit figurine

INTERIOR DESIGN

Comfort and good taste are all that the Rabbit demands in its home life, and it likes to create a classic home environment.

Soft cushion

RESTING RABBIT

This exquisite, Chinese figurine of a resting rabbit dates from the T'ang dynasty (618–906).

SYMBOLISM

*Each astrological animal is linked with a certain food,
direction, colour, emotion, association, and symbol. The
Rabbit is also associated with the season of spring.*

COLOUR

In China, green is the colour of spring, happiness, and
inner peace. Green is also the colour that is associated
with the Rabbit. This verdigris Chinese fitting is from
the Chou dynasty (c. 1100BC–901BC).

**Chinese fitting
with rabbits**

FOOD

*There are five tastes according to
Chinese astrology – salty, acrid,
bitter, sour, and sweet. Sour
foods, such as cranberries, are
linked with the Rabbit.*

Cranberries

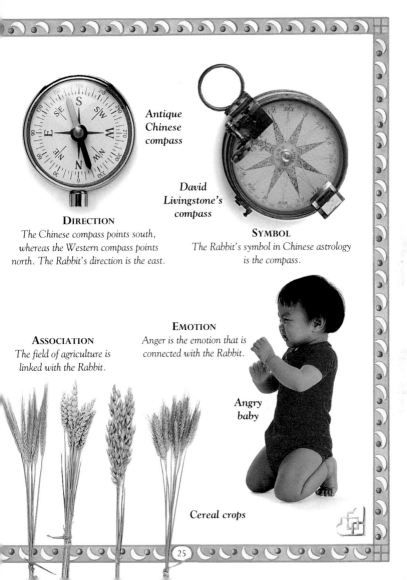

Antique Chinese compass

David Livingstone's compass

DIRECTION
The Chinese compass points south, whereas the Western compass points north. The Rabbit's direction is the east.

SYMBOL
The Rabbit's symbol in Chinese astrology is the compass.

ASSOCIATION
The field of agriculture is linked with the Rabbit.

EMOTION
Anger is the emotion that is connected with the Rabbit.

Angry baby

Cereal crops

BUDDHA RABBIT

~ 1915 1975 ~

In Chinese mythology, there are many Rabbits who gave their lives for Buddhist saints and deities. Reputedly, the Buddha was a Rabbit in a previous life.

In the West, the Rabbit tends to be considered a fluffy, slightly weak animal, and is a favourite children's pet. In China, however, the Rabbit enjoys considerable status, and is highly regarded. It is perceived as being a particularly strong and determined animal.

THE RABBIT AND THE BUDDHA

There are many powerful links between the Rabbit and the Buddha in Chinese belief, and consequently, those born in the year of the Buddha Rabbit should consider themselves fortunate. You are likely to be a highly skilled individual, well organized, and always prepared for the unexpected.

PERSONALITY

You are associated with fulfilment, and have a powerful, auspicious personality. You invariably know exactly what you want from life and deliberately set out to achieve your goals. Your determination should serve you well, and you are always likely to achieve the majority of your goals in life.

All Buddha Rabbits are highly likely to be stubborn. This can be both an asset and a problem. If you can control your tendency to be difficult, you should find that life is considerably more enjoyable, both for you and for other people.

FEMALE CHARACTERISTICS

Because of the calming effects of the yin influence, the female Buddha Rabbit can expect to enjoy a long, fulfilled life.

She is likely to be a leader or pioneer, and probably possesses immense energy. This energy should carry her to success, as well as ensuring her longevity.

Buddha Rabbit

CAREER

The goals and desires of Buddha Rabbits are not necessarily selfish. Like the Buddha himself, you are often philanthropic. Instead of seeking personal power, wealth, and success in your career, you try to direct your innate skills and forcefulness towards those who are less fortunate than yourself.

You tend to be more than willing to fight for causes that are close to your heart, and will risk being unpopular to achieve your aims. Your intelligence and powers will invariably help you to succeed.

Other people are often highly impressed by your principled stand, or sheer determination against the odds. You may find that people in authority will offer you help, and this should never be refused.

FRIENDSHIPS

Given the opportunity, you tend to always make the best of any situation. However, when exploiting your opportunities, try to ensure that this is not at other people's expense. If you allow yourself to go too far, you could eventually lose your friends' love and respect.

RABBIT LOOKING AT THE MOON

~ 1927 1987 ~

The Moon is an auspicious sign to have as a Rabbit. When the Chinese look at the Full Moon, they see a Rabbit grinding the Pill of Immortality.

You are associated with strength of character and endurance. People tend to trust you implicitly, and look up to you. Using all your skills, you do your job thoroughly.

PERSONALITY

You are equally at ease with either the intellectual or the technical, and do not shine in any one field. Instead, you tend to be a gifted all-rounder, and are valued for your willingness to become a part of whatever is happening around you.

You take immense pride in your appearance, and are blessed with excellent dress sense. This love of appearances extends to the places in which you live and work. You need an attractive working environment, and your home must be a place where everyone feels relaxed and aesthetically pleased.

FEMALE CHARACTERISTICS

The female Rabbit Looking at the Moon can sometimes be accused of being temperamental. There is an element of truth in this accusation, but if she manages to balance her skills with her frustration, her generous nature should dominate.

Nevertheless, she should make every effort to curb her tendency towards excessive complaining or grumbling. She is always likely to be respected for her skills, for they are considerable, but she may be resented, and will probably be considered irritating, if she stirs up too much trouble.

CAREER

Work is never a problem for Rabbits born in these years. They are skilful and versatile, and should always be in considerable demand.

Rabbit Looking at the Moon

FRIENDSHIPS

You are linked with the nail, symbolizing that you are the pivot to much of what goes on around you. Like most Rabbits, you invariably inspire good friendships.

RELATIONSHIPS

In emotional matters, any Rabbit Looking at the Moon should make a very good partner for the right person. This is because you have high standards, and are enjoyable company. You are usually well balanced, do not take offence easily, and have a forgiving nature.

Do try to watch out for the odd flash of temper, however, because it can be damaging, not least because it is so unexpected. As long as you are always quick to apologize, all should eventually turn out well.

RABBIT RUNNING OUT OF THE FOREST

~ 1939 1999 ~

The Rabbit Running Out of the Forest is a nervous creature.
It rarely wishes to emphasize its individuality, and is
happiest in the security of a large group.

You are associated with the interweaving of a thread through cloth. Symbolically, this means that you always want to be part of what is going on around you, and to have a clear place within it.

PERSONALITY

You are sometimes considered to be a curious Rabbit – nervous, and easily startled by anything out of the ordinary. Your highly developed sense of alarm makes you anxious and prone to feelings of unease. All Rabbits loathe disagreement and argument, but you tend to dislike them even more than most.

You are scared and worried if you find yourself pulled out of context, or standing out above the rest. You are happiest when you are part of the flow of life, and can quietly pursue your own interests.

EDUCATION

Throughout your life it is likely that you will be successful, but not to any outstanding extent. At school, your teachers probably recognized that you were a good student, but were essentially part of the crowd.

CAREER

Your career may follow a similar pattern – you never want to be perceived as an individualistic highflyer. However, it is possible that you will rise to high positions because of your natural willingness to be an integral part of a team, company, or group.

It is unlikely that you will attain a highly exalted position, however, because this goes against your wish to be part of the general flow of life. You will have increased authority and wealth, though, if you can

Rabbit Running Out of the Forest

continue to operate as part of a team, and manage not to panic when you experience difficulties.

RELATIONSHIPS

In emotional matters, it would perhaps be better for you to choose a partner who is older than you. An older partner will help to reassure you, and to make you feel more secure and loved.

Because you do not take unnecessary risks, and do not relish the strain of doing things alone, it is likely that you will have a long, fulfilled life, and a happy committed relationship. You are likely to have a full social life, and your innate friendliness and enjoyment of beautiful things will ensure that others will always feel comfortable and relaxed around you.

FAMILY

Do not be surprised if you have problems with your parents, since they may sometimes find it difficult to understand your personality. As long as you stay calm, however, they should be able to treat you as an adult, and you will all enjoy a fulfilling relationship.

RABBIT IN THE BURROW

~ 1951 2011 ~

According to appearances, this is a perfectly happy Rabbit,
because it is comfortable and secure in its natural habitat.
The burrow, however, can also represent confinement.

You are often anxious and insecure, even when you may seem to have few problems. You find it hard to accept what you have at the present moment, and are anxious about what the future might bring.

When you should be feeling relaxed and happy, you frequently find yourself caught up with trivial anxieties. You probably feel this way because you are associated with causing offence and the resulting punishment. Try to relax and enjoy the security of being a Rabbit in the Burrow instead.

PERSONALITY

Your inner tensions can sometimes make you seem rather blunt – you find it hard to be polite, and give your truthful, honest opinion when asked. This trait can often be a virtue, but if it gets mixed up with your personal anxieties, then it can become aggressive. Try to control this characteristic, and take a little time to think before you speak.

If you distinguish between what is worth saying and what comes to your mind, you are likely to gain a valuable reputation for wisdom.

RELATIONSHIPS

You should have a good committed relationship with your partner, but you must learn to control yourself, and develop your self-confidence.

You have the potential to sustain a long relationship, even though both you and your partner may have to honestly face any fears and worries that lurk below the surface.

FAMILY

At first, your family are likely to disapprove of your choice of partner, but do not worry unduly. You should find that if you are patient,

Rabbit in the Burrow

and give them enough time to make up their own minds, then they are more likely to accept, and like, your choice. Try not to hurry them, for they will invariably come round to your line of thinking.

PROSPECTS

Once you have managed to curb the acerbic side of your personality successfully, and have healthily processed your inner tensions, you should find that your life is both rich and rewarding.

You tend to have a fierce sense of independence, and whether you are at school, work, or leisure, people in positions of authority are likely to further your many interests and offer you their genuine support. As you get older, this support should bring you increasing good fortune.

RABBIT RUNNING IN THE FOREST

~ 1903 1963 ~

The Rabbit Running in the Forest has a good life. It is safe from predators, and can find plenty of food and shelter. This points to a very successful personality.

The Chinese believe in ancestor worship – that is, if their ancestors are not given due respect, then they can make life difficult for their unruly descendants.

The Rabbit Running in the Forest is particularly associated with ancestor worship. This means that, at times, if you fail to be thoughtful and considerate, life can be extremely hard – your behaviour is upsetting your dead ancestors, and they are making you suffer as a result.

Luckily, this association can also have a positive influence – if you think of others as well as yourself, then the benefits of such worthy actions are considerable.

PERSONALITY
You have the potential for success and happiness in work, leisure, and family relationships. This is largely dependent upon how you deal with others, however. Always try to remember other people, in particular those who are less fortunate than you, and those who could wield some influence over your life.

Because you can often turn difficulty into success, you can sometimes seem unsympathetic to those who find life harder. If you try to develop your charitable instincts, you should find that you become a much better person, and other people will enjoy being around you even more.

YOUTH
Invariably, it takes some time for you to realize the need to balance your own sense of confidence with some thought for others. In your youth, you are likely to find that you do not do quite as well as you expect.

34

Rabbit Running in the Forest

Undoubtedly you have the potential for success, but somehow it keeps being frustrated.

Be patient, and do not give in to feelings of despair. By learning to consider other people and by listening to the wisdom of those in authority, you will find that advancement and success will invariably be achieved as you mature.

CAREER
People in authority can have a greatly beneficial impact both on your career and on your life. Always remember to be dutiful and respectful, even though you may sometimes feel that the world is your oyster.

RELATIONSHIPS
This is also true in regard to your personal relationships. You are likely to be an extremely attractive and attentive person, but you need to beware of occasional feelings of complacency and self-satisfaction. Once you have found the right partner, however, you should be able to enjoy a very long and happy committed relationship together.

YOUR CHINESE MONTH OF BIRTH

Find the table with your year of birth, and see where your birthday falls. For example, if you were born on 30 August 1951, you were born in Chinese month 7.

1 You are clever and calm. You inspire friendship and respect, but shun fame and lavish fortune.

2 You are naturally cautious. Try to take risks in order to make the most of your opportunities.

3 You are singleminded, but should not ignore the potential richness of a more varied life.

4 You tend to overvalue yourself, and to despise less successful people. Learn to accept criticism.

5 You are morally courageous, and decisive. These qualities allow you to be at peace with yourself.

6 You combine enthusiasm with pragmatism, and optimism with realism. Success should be yours.

7 You are sensible, popular, but rather too cautious. Learn to follow your sense of intuition instead.

8 You tend to be too hasty when you make decisions, but can easily change misfortune to good fortune.

9 You may seem uncaring and hard, but your feelings for other people are deep. Learn to express yourself in order to achieve success.

10 You are spontaneous, generous, and have a tendency to make dramatic gestures. Try to relax.

11 You are thoughtful, caring, trustworthy, and a good judge of character. Your wisdom should ensure a successful future.

12 You are complex – outwardly calm, but in turmoil within. Learn to control your inner forces.

* Some Chinese years contain double months:	
1963: Month 4	1987: Month 6
24 April – 22 May	26 June – 25 July
23 May – 20 June	26 July – 23 Aug

1903	
29 Jan – 26 Feb	1
27 Feb – 28 March	2
29 March – 26 April	3
27 April – 26 May	4
27 May – 24 June	5
24 July – 22 Aug	6
23 Aug – 20 Sept	7
21 Sept – 19 Oct	8
20 Oct – 18 Nov	9
19 Nov – 18 Dec	10
19 Dec – 16 Jan 1904	11
17 Jan – 15 Feb	12

1915	
14 Feb – 15 March	1
16 March – 13 April	2
14 April – 13 May	3
14 May – 12 June	4
13 June – 11 July	5
12 July – 10 Aug	6
11 Aug – 8 Sept	7
9 Sept – 8 Oct	8
9 Oct – 6 Nov	9
7 Nov – 6 Dec	10
7 Dec – 4 Jan 1916	11
5 Jan – 2 Feb	12

1927	
2 Feb – 3 March	1
4 March – 1 April	2
2 April – 30 April	3
1 May – 30 May	4
31 May – 28 June	5
29 June – 28 July	6
29 July – 26 Aug	7
27 Aug – 25 Sept	8
26 Sept – 24 Oct	9
25 Oct – 24 Nov	10
24 Nov – 23 Dec	11
24 Dec – 22 Jan 1928	12

1939	
19 Feb – 20 March	1
21 March – 19 April	2
20 April – 18 May	3
19 May – 16 June	4
17 June – 16 July	5
17 July – 14 Aug	6
15 Aug – 12 Sept	7
13 Sept – 12 Oct	8
13 Oct – 10 Nov	9
11 Nov – 10 Dec	10
11 Dec – 8 Jan 1940	11
9 Jan – 7 Feb	12

1951	
6 Feb – 7 March	1
8 March – 5 April	2
6 April – 5 May	3
6 May – 4 June	4
5 June – 3 July	5
4 July – 2 Aug	6
3 Aug – 31 Aug	7
1 Sept – 30 Oct	8
1 Oct – 29 Oct	9
30 Oct – 28 Nov	10
29 Nov – 27 Dec	11
28 Dec – 26 Jan 1952	12

1963	
25 Jan – 23 Feb	1
24 Feb – 24 March	2
25 March – 23 April	3
See double months box	4
21 June – 20 July	5
21 July – 18 Aug	6
19 Aug – 17 Sept	7
18 Sept – 16 Oct	8
17 Oct – 15 Nov	9
16 Nov – 15 Dec	10
16 Dec – 14 Jan 1964	11
15 Jan – 12 Feb	12

1975	
11 Feb – 12 March	1
13 March – 11 April	2
12 April – 10 May	3
11 May – 9 June	4
10 June – 8 July	5
9 July – 6 Aug	6
7 Aug – 5 Sept	7
6 Sept – 4 Oct	8
5 Oct – 2 Nov	9
3 Nov – 2 Dec	10
3 Dec – 31 Dec	11
1 Jan – 30 Jan 1976	12

1987	
29 Jan – 27 Feb	1
28 Feb – 28 March	2
29 March – 27 April	3
28 April – 26 May	4
27 May – 25 June	5
See double months box	6
24 Aug – 22 Sept	7
23 Sept – 22 Oct	8
23 Oct – 20 Nov	9
21 Nov – 20 Dec	10
21 Dec – 18 Jan 1988	11
19 Jan – 16 Feb	12

1999	
16 Feb – 17 March	1
18 March – 15 April	2
16 April – 14 May	3
15 May – 13 June	4
14 June – 12 July	5
13 July – 10 Aug	6
11 Aug – 9 Sept	7
10 Sept – 8 Oct	8
9 Oct – 7 Nov	9
8 Nov – 7 Dec	10
8 Dec – 6 Jan 2000	11
7 Jan – 4 Feb	12

YOUR CHINESE YEAR OF BIRTH

Your astrological animal corresponds to the Chinese year of your birth. It is the single most important key in the quest to unlock your Chinese horoscope.

Find your Western year of birth in the left-hand column of the chart. Your Chinese astrological animal is on the same line as your year of birth, in the right-hand column of the chart. If you were born in the beginning of the year, check the middle column of the chart carefully. For example, if you were born in 1964, you might assume that you belong to the Year of the Dragon. However, if your birthday falls before 13 February, you belong to the Year of the Rabbit.

1900	31 Jan – 18 Feb 1901	Rat	1917	23 Jan – 10 Feb 1918	Snake
1901	19 Feb – 7 Feb 1902	Ox	1918	11 Feb – 31 Jan 1919	Horse
1902	8 Feb – 28 Jan 1903	Tiger	1919	1 Feb – 19 Feb 1920	Ram
1903	29 Jan – 15 Feb 1904	Rabbit	1920	20 Feb – 7 Feb 1921	Monkey
1904	16 Feb – 3 Feb 1905	Dragon	1921	8 Feb – 27 Jan 1922	Rooster
1905	4 Feb – 24 Jan 1906	Snake	1922	28 Jan – 15 Feb 1923	Dog
1906	25 Jan – 12 Feb 1907	Horse	1923	16 Feb – 4 Feb 1924	Pig
1907	13 Feb – 1 Feb 1908	Ram	1924	5 Feb – 23 Jan 1925	Rat
1908	2 Feb – 21 Jan 1909	Monkey	1925	24 Jan – 12 Feb 1926	Ox
1909	22 Jan – 9 Feb 1910	Rooster	1926	13 Feb – 1 Feb 1927	Tiger
1910	10 Feb – 29 Jan 1911	Dog	1927	2 Feb – 22 Jan 1928	Rabbit
1911	30 Jan – 17 Feb 1912	Pig	1928	23 Jan – 9 Feb 1929	Dragon
1912	18 Feb – 5 Feb 1913	Rat	1929	10 Feb – 29 Jan 1930	Snake
1913	6 Feb – 25 Jan 1914	Ox	1930	30 Jan – 16 Feb 1931	Horse
1914	26 Jan – 13 Feb 1915	Tiger	1931	17 Feb – 5 Feb 1932	Ram
1915	14 Feb – 2 Feb 1916	Rabbit	1932	6 Feb – 25 Jan 1933	Monkey
1916	3 Feb – 22 Jan 1917	Dragon	1933	26 Jan – 13 Feb 1934	Rooster

1934	14 Feb – 3 Feb 1935	Dog	1971	27 Jan – 14 Feb 1972	Pig
1935	4 Feb – 23 Jan 1936	Pig	1972	15 Feb – 2 Feb 1973	Rat
1936	24 Jan – 10 Feb 1937	Rat	1973	3 Feb – 22 Jan 1974	Ox
1937	11 Feb – 30 Jan 1938	Ox	1974	23 Jan – 10 Feb 1975	Tiger
1938	31 Jan – 18 Feb 1939	Tiger	1975	11 Feb – 30 Jan 1976	Rabbit
1939	19 Feb – 7 Feb 1940	Rabbit	1976	31 Jan – 17 Feb 1977	Dragon
1940	8 Feb – 26 Jan 1941	Dragon	1977	18 Feb – 6 Feb 1978	Snake
1941	27 Jan – 14 Feb 1942	Snake	1978	7 Feb – 27 Jan 1979	Horse
1942	15 Feb – 4 Feb 1943	Horse	1979	28 Jan – 15 Feb 1980	Ram
1943	5 Feb – 24 Jan 1944	Ram	1980	16 Feb – 4 Feb 1981	Monkey
1944	25 Jan – 12 Feb 1945	Monkey	1981	5 Feb – 24 Jan 1982	Rooster
1945	13 Feb – 1 Feb 1946	Rooster	1982	25 Jan – 12 Feb 1983	Dog
1946	2 Feb – 21 Jan 1947	Dog	1983	13 Feb – 1 Feb 1984	Pig
1947	22 Jan – 9 Feb 1948	Pig	1984	2 Feb – 19 Feb 1985	Rat
1948	10 Feb – 28 Jan 1949	Rat	1985	20 Feb – 8 Feb 1986	Ox
1949	29 Jan – 16 Feb 1950	Ox	1986	9 Feb – 28 Jan 1987	Tiger
1950	17 Feb – 5 Feb 1951	Tiger	1987	29 Jan – 16 Feb 1988	Rabbit
1951	6 Feb – 26 Jan 1952	Rabbit	1988	17 Feb – 5 Feb 1989	Dragon
1952	27 Jan – 13 Feb 1953	Dragon	1989	6 Feb – 26 Jan 1990	Snake
1953	14 Feb – 2 Feb 1954	Snake	1990	27 Jan – 14 Feb 1991	Horse
1954	3 Feb – 23 Jan 1955	Horse	1991	15 Feb – 3 Feb 1992	Ram
1955	24 Jan – 11 Feb 1956	Ram	1992	4 Feb – 22 Jan 1993	Monkey
1956	12 Feb – 30 Jan 1957	Monkey	1993	23 Jan – 9 Feb 1994	Rooster
1957	31 Jan – 17 Feb 1958	Rooster	1994	10 Feb – 30 Jan 1995	Dog
1958	18 Feb – 7 Feb 1959	Dog	1995	31 Jan – 18 Feb 1996	Pig
1959	8 Feb – 27 Jan 1960	Pig	1996	19 Feb – 6 Feb 1997	Rat
1960	28 Jan – 14 Feb 1961	Rat	1997	7 Feb – 27 Jan 1998	Ox
1961	15 Feb – 4 Feb 1962	Ox	1998	28 Jan – 15 Feb 1999	Tiger
1962	5 Feb – 24 Jan 1963	Tiger	1999	16 Feb – 4 Feb 2000	Rabbit
1963	25 Jan – 12 Feb 1964	Rabbit	2000	5 Feb – 23 Jan 2001	Dragon
1964	13 Feb – 1 Feb 1965	Dragon	2001	24 Jan – 11 Feb 2002	Snake
1965	2 Feb – 20 Jan 1966	Snake	2002	12 Feb – 31 Jan 2003	Horse
1966	21 Jan – 8 Feb 1967	Horse	2003	1 Feb – 21 Jan 2004	Ram
1967	9 Feb – 29 Jan 1968	Ram	2004	22 Jan – 8 Feb 2005	Monkey
1968	30 Jan – 16 Feb 1969	Monkey	2005	9 Feb – 28 Jan 2006	Rooster
1969	17 Feb – 5 Feb 1970	Rooster	2006	29 Jan – 17 Feb 2007	Dog
1970	6 Feb – 26 Jan 1971	Dog	2007	18 Feb – 6 Feb 2008	Pig